ALEXANDRIA OCASIO-CORTEZ FROM A TO Z

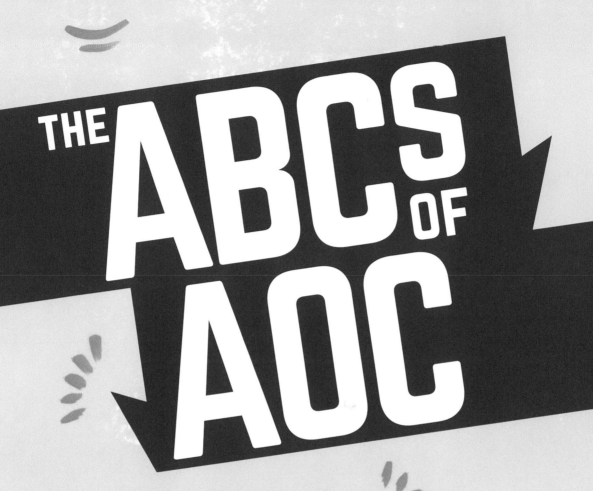

THE ABCS OF AOC

Jamia Wilson

Illustrated by
Krystal Quiles

Little, Brown and Company

New York Boston

Introduction

I was still in elementary school when I moved from the kids' corner to the adult table at our family gatherings. I loved to discuss politics with people in charge. At one of these gatherings when I was ten, an elder told my parents, "Children should be seen and not heard." That I should "learn my place."

The room was silent until the host of the celebration said, "May she never know her place. Encourage young people; they know the way forward."

That wasn't the last time I would be hushed in front of older people, but I never forgot the host's encouraging words. They immediately came to mind in 2018 when underdog Alexandria "AOC" Ocasio-Cortez, a twenty-nine-year-old Latinx native of the Bronx, beat a well-known, ten-term politician to become the youngest congresswoman in US history. AOC was clearly a woman who believed in being seen and heard—and had a lot of valuable things to say.

Ocasio-Cortez captured the public's attention with a grassroots movement and a bold message about making big changes to help immigrants, seniors, the unemployed, the uninsured, and the environment, among others. Whether people agree with her or not, her courage, fresh ideas, and outspokenness make an impression, and they may just be changing the rules of politics for the next generation of leaders.

In this book, you'll get to know AOC's world by learning about the issues she fights for, the people she represents, the political system she works in, and the qualities that many see in her, from A to Z. As you gain insight into AOC and her story, maybe you'll discover ways in which *you* can use your unique voice to plant seeds of change in your community today and in the future.

—Jamia Wilson

Advocate

As an advocate for the people of her community, Representative Alexandria Ocasio-Cortez works to enact laws that will change lives for the better.

Bronx

AOC was born in the Bronx, a part (or "borough")
of New York City, and now she represents a section
of the Bronx in Congress.

Congress

Congress is the legislative branch of the US government. Representatives from every state meet at the Capitol in Washington, DC, to make laws.

Democracy

In a democracy, people use their vote as their voice to elect people to represent them in government.

Education

Through teachers, books, and new experiences, education provides students with tools and information to help them mature and succeed.

Feminist

Feminists believe all people, regardless of gender, deserve equal rights, treatment, and access to opportunities.

Grassroots

Grassroots activism starts on the ground, in neighborhoods, when everyday people work together to make change in their community.

Human rights

Equal treatment under the law, freedom, and safety are among the basic human rights that people are born with, regardless of their age, race, ethnicity, religion, gender, or opinions.

Immigration

Immigration is coming into a new country to live there permanently.

Jobs

AOC believes that the government should guarantee fair-paying jobs to people looking to put their skills, time, and energy to use.

Knowledge

The knowledge people gain from their education and life experiences helps them solve problems and empowers them to stand up for their beliefs.

Latinx

Latinx is a gender-neutral term for people of Latin American heritage, like AOC, who is Puerto Rican.

Media

AOC uses the media—the Internet, newspapers and magazines, television and radio—to educate the public and bring attention to issues she cares about.

Nonconformist

AOC often chooses her own path instead of following other people's ideas of how things should be done, and this makes her a nonconformist.

Opponents

The two main political parties in America—the Democrats and Republicans—often have different beliefs and goals that put them on opposing sides of issues.

Protests

People join together at public protests to show their disapproval of injustices.

Queens

AOC's congressional district includes part of Queens, another of New York City's five boroughs, famous for being the most ethnically diverse urban area in the world.

Revolutionary

A revolutionary fights for fundamental change; AOC is pressing for dramatic transformations in health care, immigration, and environmental policies.

Science

AOC's first passion was science, and today it informs her views on climate change and health care for all people.

Teamwork

Teamwork enables people to reach a common goal. AOC was sworn into Congress alongside a record number of newly elected women, many of whom continue to vocally support one another.

Underdog

An underdog is someone who isn't expected to win a competition due to starting off at a disadvantage, like AOC when she won a primary race against a better-funded and better-known congressman.

Visionary

A visionary is a creative thinker who imagines a different future.

Washington, DC

Washington, DC, is the capital of the
United States and the center of
American politics and government.

Xenophobia

Xenophobia is the fear and hatred of strangers or foreigners. AOC uses her position in Congress to speak out against hate and discrimination.

"Give me your tired, your poor,
Your huddled masses
yearning to breathe free,
The wretched refuse of
your teeming shore.
Send these, the homeless,
tempest-tost to me,
I lift my lamp beside
the golden door!"

—Emma Lazarus

Youth

At twenty-nine years old, AOC is the youngest woman elected to Congress, and her youth informs her ideas for solving problems that will affect the next generation.

Zeal

Zeal is the energy and excitement that fuel activists like AOC as they strive for their goals and chase their vision of a better world.

THE A–Z OF THE ABCS: LEARN MORE ABOUT AOC

ADVOCATE: In the halls of Congress, AOC promotes social, economic, and racial equality, sharing her ideas for progress and opposing policies that block her vision.

AOC supports a progressive platform that includes equal access to housing, treating housing as a human right, and a Green New Deal program to tackle climate change.

BRONX: The northernmost of the five boroughs that make up New York City, the "boogie-down Bronx" has a long musical heritage, with a strong connection to hip-hop and Latin music. Many famous artists call this borough home. It houses the Yankees' baseball stadium and the world-renowned Bronx Zoo.

AOC lived with her family in the Bronx's Parkchester neighborhood until she was five years old. She moved back after she graduated from college. Six weeks after she took the oath of office, she thanked her hometown with a second swearing-in ceremony at a Bronx high school, where she spoke about her plans for a Green New Deal and immigration.

CONGRESS: The US Congress has two chambers, the Senate and the House of Representatives. Each state has two senators and at least one representative; the number of representatives for each state is determined by the size of its population. There are 100 senators and 435 representatives.

AOC is a member of the House and advocates for the needs and interests of her constituents, the people who live in the eastern Bronx and north-central Queens. In addition to making laws, members of Congress oversee and investigate how the nation's laws are carried out. When lawmakers like Ocasio-Cortez aren't in Washington, they are often in their home areas, listening to the concerns of the people they serve.

DEMOCRACY: Democratic government is intended to give the people supreme power. The United States is a representative democracy, where elections are held to choose the president, senators, and representatives, who all stand in for the people in making the decisions of government. America's two-party system means most voters choose between Democratic and Republican candidates.

AOC is a member of the Democratic Party but also belongs to the Democratic Socialists of America, a political organization that wants working people to democratically run the economy and society. She was one of two Democratic Socialists to win a seat in Congress in 2018.

EDUCATION: In 2019, AOC spoke at a town hall in Queens about the hurdles her father overcame to obtain the education that helped him provide for his family. She spoke of her parents' decision to move away from their Bronx community, where so many neighbors shared her family's Latinx culture, so that she could attend better schools. AOC went to a school where most of the students didn't look like her or speak Spanish. The experience inspired her to fight for education equality for all children, no matter where they live or how much money their parents make.

AOC graduated from Boston University, where she studied science before switching to economics and international relations. In Congress, she supports tuition-free public college and education access for all.

FEMINIST: A feminist believes in social, political, cultural, and economic equality for all people. Engraved over the front doors of the US Supreme Court is EQUAL JUSTICE UNDER LAW, but many classes of people, including women, still don't experience equality in treatment, pay, or civil rights. AOC supports the Equal Rights Amendment, a proposed amendment to the US Constitution stating that civil rights cannot be denied on the basis of sex.

At the 2019 Women's March, she joined thousands of demonstrators who carried signs advocating for women's health, equal pay for equal work, and keeping immigrant families together. AOC took the stage and asked, "Are you all ready to make a ruckus? Are you all ready to fight for our rights? Are you all ready to say that in the United States of America, everyone is loved, everyone deserves justice, and everyone deserves equal protection and prosperity in our country?"

GRASSROOTS: Grassroots campaigns are driven directly by people in the neighborhood, rather than by remote authority figures. Around the world, grassroots activists spread their message by knocking on doors and talking to people face-to-face, circulating petitions, and holding meetings and demonstrations. Through word of mouth and social media, grassroots campaigns bring people together to speak with one loud voice.

AOC used a grassroots campaign to win her seat in Congress. Through community-driven organizing, collecting small donations from everyday people, and inspiring youths and people of color to show up at the polls, Ocasio-Cortez beat a top-ranking incumbent and made history.

HUMAN RIGHTS: All people are born equal in rights and dignity, although laws don't always recognize this. Basic rights include equality, education, and an adequate standard of living, including access to jobs, food, shelter, and health care.

AOC is outspoken about violations to human rights. She has rallied for immigrant families to be kept together at the southern border of the United States, amplified her voice against hate and discrimination, and spoken out against people who harm women and girls.

I

IMMIGRATION: The majority of Americans today are not indigenous to this land and therefore have immigrant roots. Some arrived fleeing crises in their homelands or seeking new opportunities, while the slave trade brought the ancestors of many African Americans here by force.

Today there is a debate in this country about whether immigrants who don't have documents permitting them to stay in the United States have the right to remain with their families and receive the same services as citizens. AOC's standpoint is that people who come into the United States must be treated humanely "with the dignity and respect owed to all people, regardless of citizenship status."

J

JOBS: "Anyone who is willing and able to work shouldn't struggle to find employment," AOC believes. She proposes a federal jobs guarantee that would put people to work serving their communities with a minimum wage of $15 per hour, full health care, and child and sick leave.

As a former waitress, bartender, and community organizer, AOC has experienced the scramble to keep a family afloat. So the trailblazer walks her talk. AOC announced she would pay all her staff a living wage, and pay interns $15 per hour, above minimum wage. She called for her peers on Capitol Hill to do the same.

K

KNOWLEDGE: In addition to prioritizing education, AOC has demonstrated that she believes in the power of knowledge. She consistently uses facts and data to fight back against misinformation being spread by her opponents or in the press, and comes to congressional hearings armed with information she uses to ask tough questions and demand answers.

L

LATINX: Through her Puerto Rican lineage, AOC embodies the diversity found in her constituents. As she has tweeted, "to be Puerto Rican is to be the descendant of: African Moors + slaves, Taino Indians, Spanish colonizers, Jewish refugees, and likely others." To celebrate her Afro-Latinx heritage, Ocasio-Cortez wore a braid on Capitol Hill after her election. She revealed her Jewish ancestry at a Hanukkah event.

AOC takes pride in breaking barriers to create more opportunities for leaders of color. "Women like me aren't supposed to run for office," she said at the beginning of her first campaign ad. She believes Congress needs to change so that it reflects the nation's racial, gender, and economic diversity.

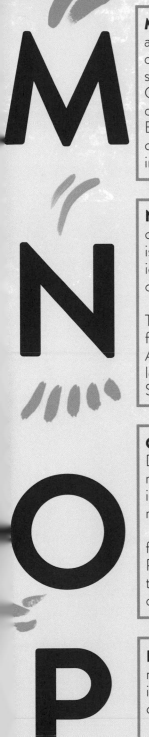

MEDIA: The media provides a worldwide communication tool, and AOC uses it as her megaphone to drive the national conversation. She has a daily presence on social media, where her tweets and Instagram posts—which range from serious to lighthearted and include behind-the-scenes looks at the workings of Congress—have made headlines and attracted a following. Traditional news outlets routinely cover her speeches and events and feature interviews with her. But just as AOC uses the media to help her cause, others use it to challenge and criticize her. *Time* magazine called her the "second most talked-about politician in America, after the President."

NONCONFORMIST: As a nonconformist, AOC resists pressure to follow the crowd, although she backs most of the viewpoints of her Democratic Party. She is one of a new generation of lawmakers making their mark with fresh policy ideas and a direct connection with the public through social media. AOC is part of a tradition-shattering Congress—the most racially and ethnically diverse ever.

AOC is also unafraid to express herself in nontraditional ways. She released a Twitter video of herself dancing into her Washington office after being criticized for dancing in a video recorded while she was in college. During her swearing-in, AOC sported bright red lipstick and hoop earrings. She said she chose her bold look to honor the Bronx native Sonia Sotomayor, the first Latinx justice of the Supreme Court, who wore red nail polish to her confirmation hearings.

OPPONENTS: The political arena in the United States is dominated by the Democratic and Republican Parties, the two organizations with the most members, money, and historic power. The two parties usually have different ideas about solving social problems, approaching taxes, and handling a wide range of national and global issues.

AOC has taken a public stand against policies that she thinks are harmful, frequently facing off with Republican opponents. Similarly, it's mostly Republican voices who criticize AOC for her outspokenness. She is sometimes the target of criticism from the White House because her ideals stand in opposition to the majority of the Republican Party's agenda.

PROTESTS: The First Amendment of the US Constitution protects citizens' right to assemble in public spaces peacefully. This form of action—which includes marches, boycotts, strikes, and other forms of resistance—has been critical throughout history in sparking cultural and political change.

AOC has participated in this tradition through the Women's March and rallies to address climate change and the fight to keep families together at the southern border. People of all ages plan and engage in protests, and many notable protest movements have been driven by young people.

Q

QUEENS: Queens is home to the country's first road built specifically for cars and the gravesite of magician Harry Houdini. So many people live in Queens that it would be the fourth-most populous city in the United States if it were separated from New York City!

AOC has recognized the city's "congressional queens" on Twitter. Bella Abzug, Shirley Chisholm, and Elizabeth Holtzman also used grassroots tactics—community organizing, going door to door, and canvassing subways—to win their seats in the House.

R

REVOLUTIONARY: While both reformers and revolutionaries seek to make a difference in their communities, they have different approaches. Revolutionaries disrupt systems that are no longer working and create new ones, while reformers work within existing frameworks to get things done. AOC is a revolutionary. She aims to transform American lives by promoting free college education, health care for all people, and a Green New Deal to address climate change and economic inequality.

S

SCIENCE: As a young person, AOC learned to use the scientific method, which involves observing, measuring, and experimenting, and testing to confirm an idea. In high school, she placed second in the world in the microbiology category at the Intel International Science and Engineering Fair. Her second-place finish won her naming rights to an asteroid.

AOC is an advocate for women in STEM (science, technology, engineering, and mathematics) fields. She made sure her four million Twitter followers knew a woman captured the first-ever image of a black hole when she congratulated computer scientist Katie Bouman: "Take your rightful seat in history, Dr. Bouman! Congratulations and thank you for your enormous contribution to the advancements of science and mankind. Here's to #WomenInSTEM!"

T

TEAMWORK: Teamwork drives AOC's work and activism. After a televised congressional hearing where she questioned the president's former lawyer, media outlets applauded her effort, calling it the "very best" and saying that other lawmakers should "watch and learn." Rather than take full credit, AOC tweeted, "Teamwork makes the dream work." Knowing that no great acts can be done alone, AOC frequently shares supportive messages about other women in Congress and joins forces with her "squad" of newly elected women of color, Representatives Ayanna Pressley, Rashida Tlaib, and Ilhan Omar. Like AOC, they were all part of a record-breaking wave of women who ran for and won seats in the 116th Congress.

UNDERDOG: In 2018, Ocasio-Cortez shocked the nation when she defeated Representative Joseph Crowley, who hadn't faced a challenger in the Democratic primary election in more than a decade. Her grassroots campaign won by promoting AOC as a newcomer to politics with original ideas and deep connections to the diverse Bronx and Queens community.

In the face of a rival with more resources and support from Democratic leadership, AOC embraced her rookie status as a strength and refused to back down. She still refuses. When President Donald Trump criticized her Green New Deal with a barb about her experience, she responded, "The last guy who underestimated me lost."

VISIONARY: Visionaries dare to consider how things *can* be instead of accepting how things are. In front of an overflowing crowd at the South by Southwest festival, AOC declared that "the greatest things we have ever accomplished as a society have been ambitious acts of vision."

She strives to bring her vision to life by pushing for creative ways to address climate change, housing access, and the economy. AOC also encourages others to think big about how to solve problems in their community without being afraid to shift or change the system. "When you see someone that is being fearful," she said, "be the person that is courageous."

WASHINGTON, DC: Washington, DC, is home to the three branches of the US government: legislative (Congress), executive (the president and Cabinet), and judicial (the Supreme Court). It is also the site of national museums and monuments and where major protests and marches have taken place.

DC stands for District of Columbia, which is bordered by the states of Maryland and Virginia. Washington, DC, is not part of either state, nor is it a state itself. The people who live and work there pay taxes but have no representative or senators in Congress. A motto on the latest DC license plates—END TAXATION WITHOUT REPRESENTATION—protests that fact. After Ocasio-Cortez moved to the nation's capital, she cosponsored a bill to make Washington, DC, a state.

XENOPHOBIA: Throughout history, there have always been people who were fearful of or hateful to "strangers" among them—people who look, sound, or act "different." Left unchecked, xenophobia can lead to damaging acts and policies. AOC has spoken out against xenophobia in her advocacy for immigrants and refugees. She is "committed to policies that make American lives better" and "not calling anyone names."

Y Z

YOUTH: AOC breaks ground for young people so that they can own their political power in the world. She teamed up with the youth-led Sunrise Movement to launch the Green New Deal resolution in the House and Senate. This grassroots movement is engaging young people across the country through town halls, a road tour, and video storytelling.

ZEAL: AOC is well known for bringing zeal to everything she does. This zeal took her to Standing Rock, North Dakota, where she joined activists blocking construction of a gas pipeline across reservation land. The enthusiasm for justice she witnessed there inspired her to run for Congress two years later, and she maintains that same zeal today.

Her lifelong passions for science and economic justice were reflected in a bold speech about the climate crisis during a Financial Services Committee hearing. Her fiery statements made headlines for communicating the urgency of the climate crisis and sparked support from a new generation of advocates.

Quote Sources

F "Are you all ready to make a ruckus?": Ocasio-Cortez, Women's March speech, New York City, Jan. 19, 2019, Global News, youtu.be/eEwHs3TM5YE.

I "with the dignity and respect owed to all people, regardless of citizenship status": Ocasio-Cortez, "Immigration Justice/Abolish ICE," platform, Alexandria Ocasio-Cortez 2018, ocasio2018.com/issues.

J "Anyone who is willing and able to work shouldn't struggle to find employment": Ocasio-Cortez, "A Federal Jobs Guarantee," platform.

L "to be Puerto Rican is to be the descendant of": Ocasio-Cortez, "Before everyone jumps," Twitter, Dec. 12, 2018, twitter.com/AOC/status/1072129158745112576.

"Women like me aren't supposed to run for office": Ocasio-Cortez, "The Courage to Change," campaign ad, May 30, 2018, youtu.be/rq3QXIVR0bs.

M "second most talked-about politician in America, after the President": Charlotte Alter, "'Change Is Closer Than We Think': Inside Alexandria Ocasio-Cortez's Unlikely Rise," *Time*, March 21, 2019, time.com/longform/Alexandria-ocasio-cortez-profile.

Q "congressional queens": Ocasio-Cortez, "People's History of Badly Behaved Women: NYC Congressional Queens Edition," Twitter, April 3, 2019, twitter.com/AOC/status/1113591689451536389.

S AOC's first passion was science: Alexandria Ocasio-Cortez, "It's true! Science was my first passion," Twitter, June 11, 2018, twitter.com/aoc/status/1006388621954506753.

"Take your rightful seat in history, Dr. Bouman!": Ocasio-Cortez, Twitter, April 10, 2019, twitter.com/AOC/status/1116078690255949824.

T calling it the "very best" and saying that other lawmakers should "watch and learn": Paul Kane, "Here's clip of @AOC questioning," Twitter, Feb. 27, 2019, twitter.com/pkcapitol/status/1100881244831825920.

"Teamwork makes the dream work": Ocasio-Cortez, Twitter, Feb. 28, 2019, twitter.com/aoc/status/1101284179088687104.

"squad" of newly elected women of color: Ocasio-Cortez, "Squad," Instagram photo, Nov. 28, 2018, www.instagram.com/p/BqGTIEPBXXD.

U "The last guy who underestimated me lost": Ramsey Touchberry, "Alexandria Ocasio-Cortez: Republican Matt Gaetz's Climate Change Proposal Is 'Weak' and 'Lame,'" *Newsweek*, April 3, 2019, www.newsweek.com/alexandria-ocasio-cortez-matt-gaetz-climate-weak-lame-1384951.

V "the greatest things we have ever accomplished as a society have been ambitious acts of vision": Ocasio-Cortez, interview by Briahna Gray, March 9, 2019, SXSW 2019, youtu.be/JU-SE5eNt04.

"When you see someone that is being fearful": Ocasio-Cortez interview by Gray.

X "policies that make American lives better" and "not calling anyone names": Ocasio-Cortez, town hall, *All In with Chris Hayes*, MSNBC, March 29, 2019, transcript, www.msnbc.com/transcripts/all-in/2019-03-29.

To my one and only mom. Thank you for teaching me to speak up, stand strong, and "get on up and keep it moving" no matter what. I'll see you in the stars. —JW

To Ma and Papi and Lyn. —KQ

About This Book

The illustrations for this book were done in mixed media and digital on 80 lb. Finch Opaque Smooth paper. This book was edited by Samantha Schutz and Lisa Yoskowitz and designed by Christina Quintero. The production was supervised by Bernadette Flinn, and the production editor was Jen Graham. The text was set in Brandon Grotesque, and the display type is Norwester.

Little, Brown and Company
Hachette Book Group
1290 Avenue of the Americas
New York, NY 10104
Visit us at LBYR.com

First Edition: October 2019

Little, Brown and Company is a division of Hachette Book Group, Inc.
The Little, Brown name and logo are trademarks of Hachette Book Group, Inc.

Library of Congress Control Number: 2019943394

ISBNs: 978-0-316-49514-1 (hardcover), 978-0-316-49522-6 (ebook), 978-0-316-49521-9 (ebook), 978-0-316-53816-9 (ebook)

Printed in the United States of America

WOR

10 9 8 7 6 5 4 3 2 1